A Turtle in the House

A Turtle in the House

John Gabriel Navarra

ILLUSTRATED BY KIYOAKI KOMODA

Doubleday & Company, Inc., Garden City, New York

Library of Congress Catalog Card Number 68–10150

A Turtle in the House

It was a warm day in July. Lisa and Jackie were out walking. They were nearing their favorite lake and they could hardly wait to go swimming!

Then they heard a sound. "Scratch, scratch, scratch."

Lisa stopped Jackie. "What was that?" she asked. They stopped and listened. The scratching sound seemed to be coming from under the ground.

They knelt down, brushed the soil away, and found little eggs hidden in the soil. They counted the eggs. There were ten of them. Jackie wondered, "How did the eggs get here?"

Each egg was about one and one half inches long. They were as white as hens' eggs. And they were leathery.

But something seemed to be happening to the eggshells! They were cracking! As the children watched, something like a little tooth poked out of one of the shells. To their amazement, the "tooth" was on a head. And the head belonged to a turtle.

The baby turtle moved its head from side to side. It was struggling to free itself from the shell. The next thing Lisa and Jackie saw were the little claws of the turtle's front feet. The claws were poked through the shell and were waving wildly. Suddenly the eggshell split, and out came the baby turtle.

The baby turtles in the other eggshells were struggling to free themselves too. They worked and rested and then worked again. Some of the turtles came out of the white leathery eggs hind feet first.

It took them a long, long time. But at last all the turtles were free.

Lisa and Jackie could see something white attached to each turtle's belly. It was part of the yolk sac. The yolk—taken from the egg—gives the baby turtle a start in the world. After the yolk is gone, the baby

turtle must hunt and find its own food. It was a surprise to find that the young turtle carried some of the yolk sac from the egg in this way. But it was no surprise to find how important this was for the turtle.

Each of the turtles had a shell. The shells were about one inch long and one inch wide. On each foot were five small webbed toes. The baby turtles looked just like grown-up turtles except that they were smaller.

As soon as they hatched, off the turtles walked. They didn't seem to have a care in the world.

The ten turtles started off toward the large lake which was close by. The lake was a big body of still water. It had a very muddy bottom. Trees and other plants ringed the lake. There were a lot of water plants close to the shore.

The baby turtles did not need to be told that the lake would be their home. They moved as fast as they could toward the lake.

Lisa and Jackie heard another sound. This time it came from above. "Caw! Caw! Caw!" They looked up. Circling above were four crows.

The crows spotted the baby turtles. The big birds swooped down and attacked them. When the birds left, Lisa and Jackie could find no turtles. They looked and looked and looked.

The children sat on a log. They were very quiet and very sad. Just a few minutes before there had been so many turtles and now there were none.

Then from beneath the log they heard a long hiss. It was not very loud. At first, they thought it might be a snake. Lisa jumped up and pulled Jackie along with her. They listened and heard it again. It was a long, low hissing sound.

Something began to move under the log. Lisa wanted to run. Jackie said, "Don't move!"

They did not know what to expect. Then to their amazement, out came one of the baby turtles.

The children were so happy. They thought all the turtles were lost. But their happiness quickly gave way to concern when Lisa asked, "What will happen if the crows return?"

Lisa picked up the turtle carefully. The turtle moved its legs back and forth as though it were trying to swim away. It was so cute and it seemed so helpless! Lisa said, "I can't leave it here."

Jackie agreed. They picked up the turtle, put it in a box, and away they went.

The children were excited when they reached home. Father heard them and asked what they had in the box. Before they could say anything, the turtle poked its head over the top of the box. It was such a funny, unexpected sight that Father laughed.

Lisa explained what had happened at the lake. Father listened and they knew he understood when Jackie said, "We want to keep the turtle and care for it."

Father agreed that it might be a good idea to care for the turtle. But he said there would come a time when the turtle would be old enough to care for it- self. "Then," he said, "you should plan to set it free."

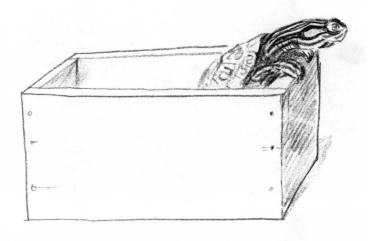

In the meantime there was a lot to do. Lisa and Jackie needed to learn about the turtle and its habits so they might properly care for it. Father agreed to help them study the turtle. They looked at the turtle's markings. They turned it over. They looked at the turtle from the top, the bottom, and the sides. Then Lisa, Jackie, and Father began to search in books. First, they looked for pictures that looked like their turtle. Father was very helpful. He explained many things to them.

Lisa and Jackie solved many puzzles about their turtle. One of the first was to find its name. They searched and found many pictures. Jackie was able to match the turtle with one of the pictures.

1	Eastern Painted	5	Northern Diamond-back
2	Midland Painted	6	Yellow-bellied
3	Western Painted	7	Peninsula Cooter
4	Southern Painted	8	Chicken Turtle

The first thing the children noticed was that their turtle had a red patch on both sides of its head. These patches give the turtle its common name. It is called a *Red-eared Turtle*.

9   Elegant Slider or Red-ear

10   Eastern Box

11   Florida Soft-shell or Southern Soft-shell

12   Eastern Spiny Soft-shell

13   Common Snapping Turtle

14   Common Musk

15   Spotted Turtle

Most turtles have common names. Sometimes they have more than one common name. For example, the red-eared turtle is also called the *Elegant Slider*.

Lisa and Jackie soon found that common names are not very reliable. It is true that almost everyone uses red-eared as the common name for this turtle. But the turtle's ear is not red. And the red patch is really above the ear!

Scientists do not like to use common names. They make up special names which are more reliable. The scientific name is always made up of two parts. The first part of the scientific name is a group name. Scientists call this group a *genus*. The second part of the name identifies an individual in the group. Scientists call this a *species* name.

Saw-tooth

Red-ear

You might say the scientific name works like your name but in reverse. Your last name tells us the family to which you belong. This is like a group name. Your first name tells which individual you are in the family group.

Three turtles are shown in the picture. Two of the turtles belong to the same group. The lower shells of the red-eared turtle and the saw-toothed turtle do not move. Their shells are fixed in place. Because of this fixed shell and other characteristics, scientists say that the red-eared and saw-toothed slider belong to the same group.

The lower shell of the box turtle has two movable sections. The movable lower shell puts the box turtle in a different group from that of the red-eared turtle.

Box

Scientists have a group name for the red-eared and saw-toothed slider. The group name is *Pseudemys*. All the turtles in this group have lower shells made up of twelve plates. And the lower shells do not move.

But these turtles have differences even though they belong to the same group. The first difference is in the pattern of the heads. This is not strange. Think of

Red-ear

Saw-tooth Turtle

your own family. You all belong to the same group but each member of your family looks a bit different!

The second difference is not easy to see because you need to look at the ridge on the upper jaw of each turtle. The ridge in the red-eared turtle is smooth, but the ridge in the other turtle is strongly toothed, and this gives it the common name of saw-toothed slider.

The red-eared turtle is given the name *Pseudemys scripta*. The scientific name for the saw-toothed slider is *Pseudemys floridana*. The first part of each name tells us these turtles belong to the same group. When we use the second part of the scientific name, we know exactly which specific kind of turtle we are talking about.

The first part of the scientific name tells us the things these turtles have in common. The second part of the name tells us the differences between them.

Knowing the name of their turtle was just a beginning. Lisa and Jackie knew they had a lot more to learn in order to care for their red-eared turtle properly.

Lisa and Jackie told Father about the hissing sound the turtle made when they found it. They thought at first it was a snake under the log. Father said that didn't surprise him because, after all, a snake and a turtle are related. They are both reptiles.

Jackie wanted to know what Father meant. "How can a snake and a turtle be related?" he exclaimed.

Father explained, "Four groups of animals, all called reptiles, had a common ancestor many millions of years ago. The four groups of animals are the turtles, crocodiles, lizards, and snakes. All of these animals are called reptiles."

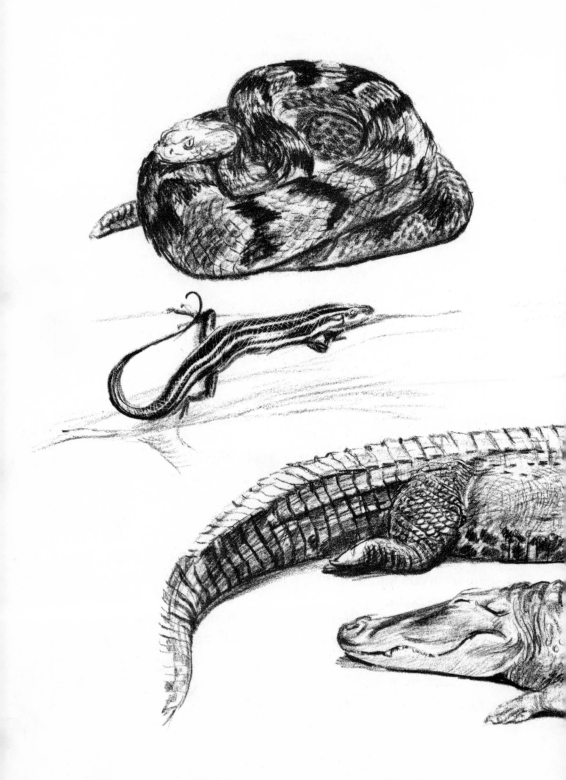

Jackie wanted to hear more about the reptiles of long ago. So Father began his story. "Millions of years ago the earth was ruled by reptiles. They roamed over the land and swam in the seas. Some even flew in the air. There were more reptiles in the world than any other animals." Father swung his arms way out as he said, "They were huge beasts."

Father used Mother's purse to show the children the skin of a modern reptile. "Do you know what this is?" he asked.

"Alligator skin!" the children shouted.

"Right," said Father. "All of the ancient reptiles had a horny skin. The skin was usually in the form of folded overlapping scales.

1	Cotylosauria	4	Sauropterygia
2	Thecodontia	5	Ichthyosauria
3	Pterosauria	6	Saurischia

3

4

5

6

"The earliest of the most primitive reptiles was called a *cotylosaur*. This primitive reptile was more than five feet in length. It had a solid, long, deep skull. It also had sharp teeth along the edge of its jaws. Its legs were strong but they seemed rather sprawly."

Jackie found a picture of a cotylosaur in an encyclopedia. They studied the picture and Father continued. "The cotylosaurs were the first reptiles. Many other reptiles descended from the early cotylosaur. Some of the reptiles lived in the sea, some lived on land, and some moved through the air.

Ornithischia (group name)

(Stegosaurus)

"The great reptiles existed over a period of more than one hundred million years. Most of these ancient reptiles have disappeared from the earth. They do not live today."

Lisa tugged on Father's arm. He could see that she was almost overcome by curiosity. "What happened to all the ancient reptiles?" she asked.

"They vanished from the earth, but there are survivors. The reptiles that are living today are the turtles, crocodiles, lizards, and snakes," Father replied. Then he added, "No one is sure why all the ancient reptiles did not survive. But we do know that conditions on the earth changed. And for some reason the largest reptiles were unable to survive in the changing world.

"Modern reptiles such as turtles, lizards, and snakes can be found all over the earth. They have been very successful in finding places to live. But today the largest living reptile is nothing but a pigmy compared with the ancient giant reptiles."

The children looked at pictures of modern reptiles.

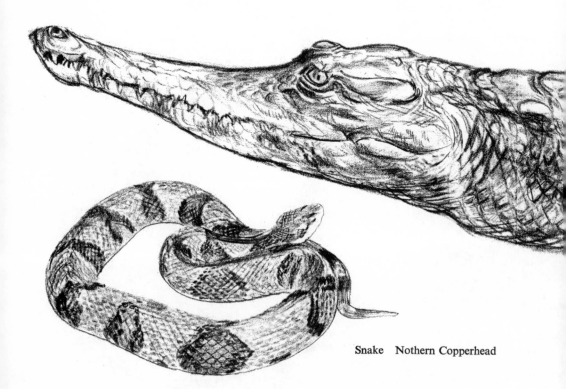

Snake   Nothern Copperhead

Lizards   Six-lined Racerunner

Turtle   Diamond-back Terrapin

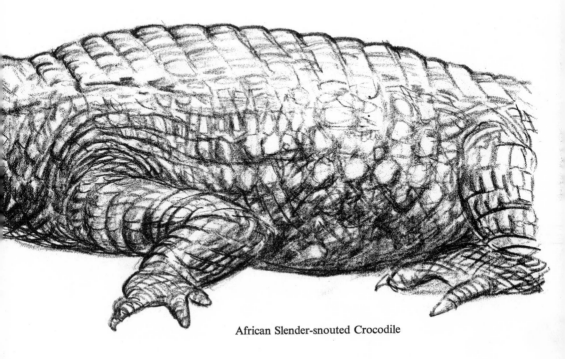

African Slender-snouted Crocodile

Lisa found many ways in which they were different from each other: "The turtle does not look at all like a snake. The snake has no legs. Turtles, lizards, and crocodiles have legs." She continued, "The turtle has a shell. The other animals in the reptile family don't have shells."

Jackie asked Father to explain why scientists say reptiles are alike.

Father helped the children to find out. He showed them that turtles, crocodiles, lizards, and snakes all have backbones. Father pointed out, "This is one important way that reptiles are alike. All reptiles have backbones.

"There is another way in which reptiles are alike," Father explained. "They all breathe air. Reptiles take air into their lungs just as you do."

Lisa was puzzled by this bit of information. She knew that some reptiles live in water. Jackie wondered if the reptiles which live in water have gills and breathe like fish. Father answered his question. "All the reptiles, even those that live in water, breathe air and have lungs. The turtle and all other reptiles must come to the surface of the water to get air and breathe."

The next day, after a trip to the school library, Lisa had important information to report to Jackie. "There is another way in which turtles, crocodiles, lizards, and snakes are alike." She ran on, "All these animals are said to be cold-blooded."

Jackie was puzzled; but Father explained, "This means reptiles do not have any set body temperature as we do. The body temperature of a man is almost 99° F. Our bodies stay at this temperature no matter what the temperature of the air is.

"A cold-blooded reptile such as a turtle will be warm or cold depending upon the temperature of the air. A turtle does not have any way of keeping its blood warm. When the air temperatures drop, a turtle and all other reptiles may be in danger. They get cold and slow down. They have difficulty moving and they are not able to eat very much.

"A turtle is able to protect itself from the cold when temperatures drop. It does this by burrowing into mud or crawling into a hole. Reptiles usually spend the winter sleeping in protected places. This winter sleep is called hibernating.

"But some reptiles live where temperatures are very high. These reptiles must protect themselves during the hot part of the day. They usually stay hidden in a cool place until the temperature drops at night. Reptiles which live in hot places move around at night.

"Remember, turtles, crocodiles, lizards, and snakes are called reptiles. They never have gills. They all have lungs to breathe air. They are all cold-blooded, and all of them have backbones."

Father asked the children if knowing that the red-eared turtle is a reptile would help them to care for it. Jackie thought for a while, then answered, "Yes!" He explained that they knew that the turtle, because it is a reptile, is cold-blooded. This meant their red-eared turtle would have little or no control over its body temperature. They had to be careful to see that the turtle did not get too cold or too hot.

Father cautioned, "Turtles do best at temperatures between 75° and 85° F. The turtles, of course, can stand much lower temperatures and much higher temperatures than these; in fact, they are normally active between 50° and 98° F. But they do best between 75° and 85° F."

The red-eared turtle normally lives in large bodies of quiet water. Lakes with low, swampy shores are favorite places for these turtles. But quiet coves or an oxbow of a larger river also provide quiet water where this turtle can be found. Small prairie ponds are another favorite home for the red-eared turtle.

In such quiet bodies of water, there are usually many water plants. The red-eared turtle lives in and around water plants.

Father explained to the children that a turtle in its natural home can live through great changes in temperature. If the red-eared turtle were out on a very hot day, it might burrow into damp leaves or bury itself in cool mud. And, of course, the water of the pond, lake, or river would help keep the turtle cool.

If the temperature were to get very cold, the turtle might find a sheltered spot and expose itself to the sun. In this way the turtle would warm up.

Jackie said he knew what the turtle would do if things got very cold. Before Father could ask, Lisa cried, "Hibernate!"

Lisa asked Father to take them on an expedition to the lake. They wanted to observe red-eared turtles out in nature. Father planned the trip carefully. And they were able to observe that out in nature the red-eared turtle spends a lot of time sunning itself. Lisa and Jackie found that in a natural home the turtle moves in and out of sunlight when it wishes—sunning itself when too cool and shading itself when too warm.

The children kept their red-eared turtle in an aquarium. They put a large rock in the aquarium for the turtle to climb on and sun itself. They also made a little shady spot so their turtle could get out of the sun.

"There are many reasons, in addition to keeping warm, for the turtle to spend time in the sun," Father explained. "The sunlight helps the turtle stay healthy. The sunlight kills many different kinds of infections which the turtle might develop. Leeches, insects, and bacteria may live in pond water. The sunlight helps kill these pests if they should attach themselves to the turtle."

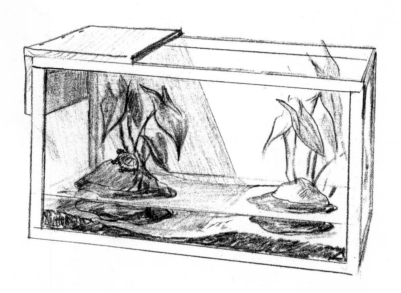

Because the turtle is a reptile, it will go into a winter sleep out in nature: Red-eared turtles stop feeding sometime in October. Over the warm months of summer they get good and fat. Plenty of food is stored up in the turtle's body. As the days grow cold and the temperatures drop, the red-eared turtle buries itself deep in the earth or in the mud under water. In order to live through the winter the turtle must burrow deep —down to a level where the temperature does not fall below 32° F.

During the winter the turtle just barely lives. Its "thermostat" for body temperature is turned way down but not below freezing. The turtle uses very little food while hibernating. It hardly breathes. In fact, it is best for the turtle to be in a place where the temperature is quite low, but not freezing. In such a cold place the fat and stored food will last throughout the winter because it will be used very slowly.

Jackie asked if the pet turtle would be able to hibernate in the aquarium in the house. But then he answered his own question when he realized the temperature would be above 70° F. Father told him to expect the turtle to stay active throughout the year. The house temperature would turn the winter into a long summer.

Lisa and Jackie made plans to feed their turtle over the winter.

In nature the red-eared turtle is a hunter. The young red-eared turtle eats meat. But at times it also eats plants. Insects and larvae are the animals eaten most frequently by the young turtles. The adult red-eared turtles eat plants also, but they eat crayfish on occasion.

Lisa and Jackie found that their turtle would eat earthworms, chopped liver, chopped beef, and fish. Their young turtle preferred meat but at times ate some water plants and small bits of lettuce.

Lisa saw that the turtle gulped food under water! Father explained, "The turtle does have a very special way of eating. It has no teeth. This lack of teeth is probably the reason it gulps food down."

Sometimes Lisa noticed that a piece of food was too big for her pet to gulp down. Then it would tear at it with its claws. Lisa tried to tell Father what the turtle did as it ate. She said the turtle seemed to comb the food. Father told Lisa that was a good description. The turtle really does tear at the food with its claws and combs the food out straight. The combing helps the turtle change the size or shape of the food so that it can be swallowed.

Tearing

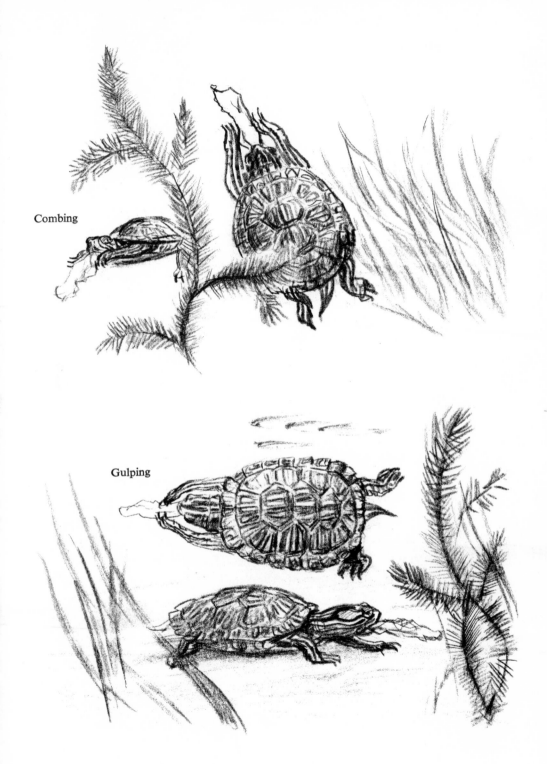

Combing

Gulping

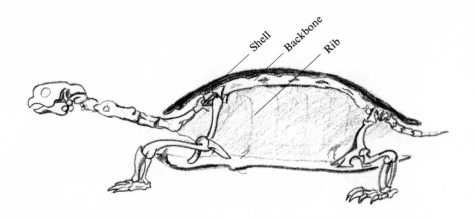

An adult turtle has a lot of bone. The red-eared turtle Lisa and Jackie had was young. It had just been born when they found it. Father told the children that their young turtle had a lot of bone to grow.

"Inside a turtle," Father said, "is a skeleton. Remember, it is a reptile and all reptiles have backbones. A turtle's backbone runs from its head to its tail.

"The bones of the backbone are called vertebrae. The joints of the neck vertebrae are very flexible. Don't forget, the turtle can move its neck all around and it also can fold it into the shell! But it is another story with the back vertebrae. These bones are fused to the bony plates of the shell. There are shoulder bones, wrist bones, and hand bones in the skeleton. Also there are hip bones, leg bones, ankle bones, and foot bones.

"The upper shell of the turtle is called a *carapace*. The lower shell is called a *plastron*. The shell of the turtle is made up of scales or horny *scutes*. Underneath these scales or scutes are strong bony plates."

Upper Shell or Carapace   Lower Shell or Plastron

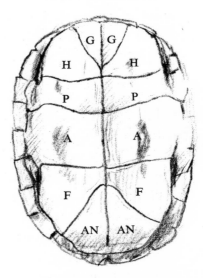

N — Nuchal   G — Gular
V — Vertebral   H — Humoral
C — Costal   P — Pectoral
M — Marginal   A — Abdominal
Pc. — Postcentrals F — Femoral
          AN — Anal

Because the turtle has a great deal of bone it needs a lot of calcium. Calcium is what bones are made of. When a turtle does not have enough calcium it usually develops sore eyes. But in addition its shell will soften.

In nature there is usually calcium in the water. In an aquarium calcium must be added to the water. The children used a lump of plaster of Paris to supply calcium to their turtle. They just dropped it in the water. Enough calcium dissolved from the plaster of Paris to give their turtle calcium.

Father told the children that the turtle also needed vitamin D. It is important and necessary for bone growth. Bones and shell soften when the turtle lacks vitamin D. When the turtle suns itself, it gets this vitamin from the sunlight.

Lisa and Jackie decided to give their turtle cod-liver oil during the wintertime. They squirted it directly into the turtle's mouth. The cod-liver oil has a lot of vitamin D in it.

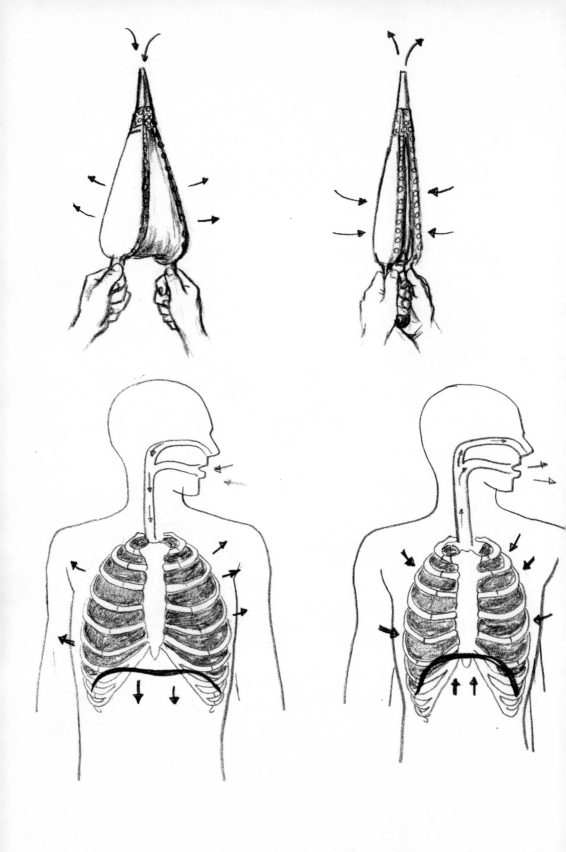

Lisa and Jackie observed many things. But one of the things that puzzled them was that their turtle swallowed a lot. Father told them that this could be the way a turtle takes in air. He explained, "The turtle cannot breathe as we do. When we take in air our ribs stretch. A turtle cannot stretch its ribs. The ribs are part of the shell and the shell is stiff. It will not give. So the turtle must have other ways to take in air. You might say a turtle pumps air into its lungs each time it swallows."

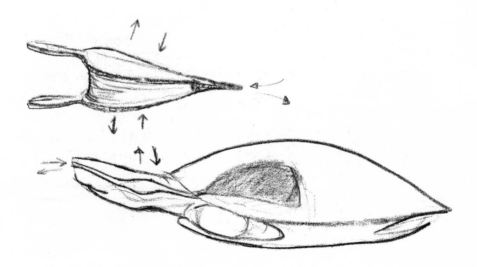

Lisa and Jackie learned that there were more than two hundred different kinds of turtles in the world. And they come in all sizes—small and large. Many turtles live in water. They are called aquatic turtles. Some of the aquatic turtles live in fresh water. Others live in salt water. Many turtles do not live in water. They live on the land. A land turtle is sometimes called a *tortoise*.

One of the best ways to tell an aquatic turtle from a land turtle is to look at the feet. A land turtle usually has a foot like an elephant. You might say the foot looks like a club. The water turtles usually have flattened feet with webbed toes. The feet of some of the large turtles which live in the sea look like swimming flippers.

In the United States and Canada there are about eighty different kinds of turtles. The red-eared turtle that Lisa and Jackie found is just one of the eighty different kinds of turtles which might be found in the United States.

Jackie and Lisa had found their turtle in July. They cared for the turtle during the fall and winter. By early spring the turtle had grown. They learned a lot about their turtle during the ten months they cared for it.

Green Turtle   (Ocean)

Sawback Turtle   (Fresh Water)

Desert Tortoise   (Land)

One day in May, Lisa and Jackie took their turtle back to the place where they found it. It was a warm pleasant day. Their turtle had grown. They had taken good care of it. They placed it carefully on the ground. And then the turtle took up the journey it had started more than ten months before. It headed for the lake to join other turtles.

Lisa and Jackie sat on the log and watched. Each of them hoped they might see the turtle again. They were sorry to see Red-Ears go, but they knew that letting him return to the wild was the proper thing to do.

JOHN GABRIEL NAVARRA, the author of A
TURTLE IN THE HOUSE, is chairman of the science
department at Jersey City State College. As both a
teacher and a writer, Dr. Navarra has an international
reputation. He was the teacher of the first televised
science course to be offered in the South when he was
on the faculty of East Carolina College. He has written
one other science book for children, *Clocks, Calendars
and Carrousels,* and he has written eight adult science
books plus several pamphlets and is the senior author
of a complete series of science books, grades kinder-
garten through nine, that are used by millions of
school children throughout the United States.

KIYOAKI KOMODA was born in Saijo, Japan,
and moved to California after finishing high school.
He studied at Los Angeles City College and at Choui-
nard Art Institute. He has illustrated a number of
children's books, including *Aluk* and *Hide-out for a
Horse,* and has drawn several jackets for young
peoples' books, including *Kirsti* and *Julie.* He has been
the art director for two adult science books and his
work has appeared in *Harper's* magazine.